MOTHERHOOD: A GHOST STORY

Anna Brook is a writer and lecturer; they recently completed a PhD in creative life writing at Kingston University. Anna's prose/poetry practice centres around the complexity and ambivalence of motherhood experience, haunting and failure, and the ways in which we attempt to express the ineffable. They have published broadly within maternal studies and as a poet. Anna is currently a guest editor of *Studies in the Maternal* journal and co-founder of the Visceral Bodies research network.

ISBN: 978-1-917617-29-1

Cover designed by Aaron Kent

Edited and Typeset by Aaron Kent

Broken Sleep Books Ltd
PO BOX 102
Llandysul
SA44 9BG

TW: This text contains mentions of suicide.

Motherhood: A Ghost Story

Anna Brook

Broken Sleep Books

Our world was quiet this morning because it had rained.

I so wanted to ask you more about what you meant—that motherhood makes you a child again yourself—because I've felt that same returning and I wanted to know if we meant the same thing, or something close at least. But I was behind you as you spoke, carrying my boots stuffed with my socks, along the edge of the beach road on the grass verge hemmed by cars. And carrying him too, wet to the chest with seawater, legs rough with sand. The seawater soaking through my T-shirt as I held him above my hip, always arching back a little, resisting, not settling his weight against mine so I could balance easily but shifting continually.

It was the first time he had been in the sea. Well I had touched his feet to the water when he was six months old, but this was his first time to explore, to feel the seaweed at his ankles, the currents, and the softness of sand beneath moving water.

I'm not sure I needed to ask you more—I could hear in your voice the shocking vulnerability of your motherhood, your being made a child again by that vulnerability, by your helplessness at the shock of continual change that we forget from childhood, when change was so frequent yet always shocking. Our grasp on time so tenuous then and the paucity of our agency as children—but I wanted to let you say more.

Instead, I sat him on the underlip of the car boot and pulled his water tightened clothes from his limbs and fumbled for the dry clothes in my bag as he prickled with goose bumps, all the time explaining that we'd come back to the sea, *next time, I promise*. You changed Theo's clothes too, and we checked the minutes left to reach the station for the train back to London, when we would leave you here.

From the start

The wooden rattle sound of a magpie.

I have this image of a ceramic vessel, spherical, pale yellow ochre, textured, which is opened by breaking. I see it in my chest, though I didn't know until now that it was there. It contained a body of emotion that now forms a well between my heart and stomach and sloshes about messily in part of the space he once pressed upon. I wonder if there is a version of this vessel in ceramic history—I would research it if I weren't so tired.

This lodged vessel, that required the precise pitch of his first cries—actually, not his first, but his first out of my arms, flailing on the kitchen table, receiving his first nappy I think—to break apart, as if dropped on stone, was not all that broke. Or, and I think maybe this is it, its contents trickled down the inside of my ribs loosening the sediment that had formed there, never terribly effectively, over my ghosts.

A few months after his birth I experienced a period of occasional hallucinations. I never really admitted them as such, even to the NHS therapist whose chair being higher than mine made me feel pleasantly/uncomfortably like a child. I declared them as *not hallucinations exactly*, but they were and she echoed them back to me without my reserve—a product of not wanting to seem *dramatic* and also a fear of the powerlessness that comes with being deemed mad. I think of author Janet Frame's near-miss with a lobotomy, and all the millions of others not saved by their own poetry.

My hands, holding my baby, were not my own, that was the hallucination. It wasn't that they felt like someone else's, but that they looked like hers. Not similar or reminiscent, but as if they were hers. It struck me with the feel of a possession or a haunting. And I am reminded, in a fashion of odd circular connectedness, of the haunting in Frame's novel *The Carpathians*—such a beautifully rendered ghostly presence, a hallucination perhaps.

I remembered, too late to share it with the tired but always engaged therapist, a moment shortly after my grandmother's death. My grandfather took my hands and told me they were like hers (a different her)—it was stifling. I'm fairly sure they are nothing like hers were, we were physically dissimilar. Perhaps he was hallucinating them, projecting them. They had spent decades in almost exclusively each other's company and were very much in love.

I liked her, this first therapist—a little odd, very present—but when she said *why should he be different?* not really as a question, I knew it was another wall. Did I answer, *why shouldn't he be?* I should have.

Perhaps it is just the effect of the well-documented sleep-deprivation that so often accompanies early parenthood, or perhaps the neurological changes that pregnancy, birth and breastfeeding bring about, but I feel more vulnerable to ghosts—mine and others'. Or perhaps I am unhinged by the terrifying normalness of this creature-person who is suddenly with me always and whose near-silent sleep I have disturbed without fail for a full 365 days, in an effort to detect his breath. *Happy birthday my darling*. The rise and fall of his ribs is so slight that to feel it I must hold my own breath while my hand rests there. Yet his existence is so powerful, and his absence so unimaginable (or sickeningly possible), I have written him in to memories from before.

A rose garden in Ohio, all bare black and winter cropped, in a blizzard. I was alone and, I seem to remember, feeling especially alone and a little desperate. But, overlaid, like a transparency, I remember my pregnant self there, a self that wouldn't come to be for more than a year, and never in Ohio.

I can't seem to lose the metaphor of haunting. Perhaps that's the thread of this, the thing that will string it together, like I planned it all along, rather than it just happening, bit by bit, as he sleeps beside or on me. But it is for you to read, so I'd like it to be okay.

In any case, this state feels something like a return to, or an accessing of, something of the world as it was to me as a child, which was most certainly haunted. Perhaps that's just the way I construct my image of the world to reflect the feeling of anxiety back to myself. This constructing of images (not ideas, but solid, concrete images) to show myself the world, or what I am feeling in it, or a way to cope, seemed new to me, but now I come to write about it I think it may be old, I think it may be something I had lost the knack for, or the habit of.

The first of these recent images came as I was giving birth, in an inflatable pool in my front room, my head and arms over the side and a towel beneath my chin to blanket the plastic smell of the pool. As I felt what I understand to be my body's 'natural expulsive reflex' pressing with unnerving force around the body I had tried to hold so gently for so long, I could see the form and colour of that force—a faceted lozenge, like a cut stone, but with all the planes roughly the same size, a colour between that of amethyst and rose quartz.

At the time, in the trippy, time-bent state of labour, this didn't seem a strange way of understanding the feeling, but the image remained and seems odd to me now. Like the token, some small object, the child finds in their pocket as proof that the fantastical world they found (through a secret door or some such) wasn't a dream after all, in that many-versioned children's story.

Leaf bare apple tree hung with chartreuse apples, rotting on the branches? Ivy clotted trees and fences.

To this day I feel unconvinced that milk passes almost entirely unseen between our bodies in quantities great enough to sustain his rapid growth. I was never one of those new mothers whose breasts leaked in the shower—he had a tongue-tie, which got things off to a halting and painful start, but I faked the faith I needed to keep going and here we are, feeding (endlessly, in his sleep, to sooth a sore ear) as I type. But I am haunted just now and then by an almost unspeakable vision where I wake from this delusion to find there was never any milk and I am the Miss Havisham of breastfeeding.

It is just a fleeting thought—like the many morbid thoughts that loving in such utter vulnerability makes inevitable, to many I think. But it has purchase in my lack of easy faith. I wonder now if I have avoided situations where this kind of faith is necessary, only to be immersed now in this life where it is so often all there is to go on.

Especially in this space before he has language. I have been cynical of language in the past, but right now it seems a glorious, glimmering hope emerging ever so slowly, as repeated sets of sounds, from silence and cries. I beg its forgiveness—I did not understand.

When he is ill the space between his expression, for I am
not sure how much of it is communication yet, and my
understanding is almost unbearable. The trial and error of
holding, setting down, holding again, of offering a breast, or the
other, preferred one, of singing, of distraction or of quiet, takes
such forceful concentration, such artificial calm. And then, in
the end, he sleeps.

And I know that the key, the answer to his demand, is never
quite the same twice, and the code is re-set. But for now he
sleeps.

In this practice of caring for him without reciprocal language, I try to observe (both to watch and to undertake) the rhythms he needs to make his way through the day. On days when he is not distraught with teething pain, the rhythms make for a gentle sort of structure and I find joy in their flow.

On difficult, pain-filled days they allow us to get from one end of the day to the other, bit by bit. They are always changing, and it is in their redundance that I most clearly feel the pace of his development. Their transitions are rarely smooth and I must try to allow enough space for the new rhythm to make itself felt, whilst mourning the slow grace we had settled into.

My hands and face became tanned from hours of steady, spring and then summer walking, through city parks and along canals, his belly pressed to my ribs, held by a fabric wrap in what (as I watched the instruction video again and again on YouTube) seemed at first an unfeasible way to secure a baby. But the vessel was broken and the sediment shifted and I was awash with ghosts and emotion that belied the *healthy glow* I had inadvertently gathered to my almost always pale skin.

For a time, before you moved to Essex and your inlet of sea, you and I, sometimes Livi too, and the babies, spent afternoons on the roof-terrace of the *posh flats* next to our housing association development. You had stopped me in the street to ask about the wrap I was using to carry him, then maybe six months old, and we fell into meeting up to walk our wakeful or sleeping babies.

You lived in the *posh flats*, in a former match factory, in a tiny space with one huge window. That summer we let our infants crawl around the roof terrace in the afternoons, hauling themselves up to their wobbly legs on the plastic furniture, when we were both too tired to take them anywhere else.

In the autumn we met one rain soaked afternoon in the posh flats' private bar/restaurant, which felt for all the world like a bar in a cheap English seaside town in the 1990s, and forged a link with a memory of a teenage camping trip to Newquay with my (much older) boyfriend and two school friends, so that now I can't think of one without the other. Sara and I collected striped pebbles on the beach, the glove compartment reeked of weed and we came home early because their tent leaked in a downpour. I watched them dance and smoke.

You felt it too, the strange effect of the place, and we joked about the small English towns we had grown up in and their dated suburban weight.

It happened again, only briefly this time, as I lifted his arm by
the wrist from where it lay, limp with sleep, across my breast,
it was as if my hand were hers. Or, and I don't understand how
this could be, it was as if I already knew that moment from both
sides; she had taken my arm by the wrist in that way and I had
known she could feel the smallness of its bones, the tension of
its tiny tendons, I had imagined what that felt like so clearly as to
feel it *as* her, because, always, I was trying to know what she felt.

And I had somehow just experienced that moment again but out
of time and implicating this third party, this unsuspecting trigger
whom my psyche, it seems, reaches out to for answers. I am
suffused with guilt; he is not here for that. Nor does this writing
make something noble or special of it. My wish is to be alone with
him without my ghosts, and mostly I am, or never, I'm not sure.

I asked to see my/his placenta, before it was disposed of.
The obliging second midwife, happy I think to be involved as
she had missed his relatively speedy birth by a few minutes,
brought a plastic bowl containing the organ to where we lay. She
proceeded, unprompted (but to my delight) to explain its parts.
I felt, strongly, the need to see it, this organ I/we had grown,
which had so suddenly become redundant and expelled. But,
oddly, I can only remember the bowl—semi-opaque, white
plastic.

As I write about it, the image begins to build back up and I
think, perhaps, I can remember it. Not in full, but its surface at
least. But I wonder if my mind is creating rather than reclaiming
the image. I think it's likely I've lost the original. I remember
a novel read many years ago, *The Autumn of the Patriarch*, and
I picture my psyche rushing about to cobble some version of
a missing placenta together to protect me from the loss, of
its image as much as of itself, like the staff of Márquez's mad
despot, faking a moon and a Turin Shroud of his dead mother,
I think.

Each time I bath him, in his evening ritual, I am referred back, without fail, to a passage from *The Waves*. It turns out it is actually not one passage, as I remembered it, but a repeating refrain. One instance reads,

Yes, ever since old Mrs Constable lifted her sponge and pouring warm water over me covered me in flesh I have been sensitive, percipient.

My experience of reading Virginia Woolf is, so often, one of vivid emotional clarity. I envy this clarity. Not in the sense that I envy her writing (though I do, the implicit yet sure nature of her language) but in that I wish I could experience my own, immediate emotional state with the crisp edges, the folds, the fullness she gives the affect of her characters.

Last year I described to the NHS therapist (the muscles just below her right eye gently twitching, with tiredness I assume, it was 6pm after all) the screen (like a light, open-weave fabric stretched taut) through which I thought I could perhaps make out my happiness, and all the rest. That feeling of being alienated from oneself, like the ghost in the 90s movie trope who finally realises it is dead and, no matter how much it wills it, cannot really be in the world. But this was not what I intended to write.

It is, I think, the ambivalence in being made to feel, in being born—or being made flesh by the water from Old Mrs Constable's sponge—that I find so affecting. As I wash him and remember *The Waves*, each time, I am thinking about how these actions—the lavender in his bath water, the soft sea sponge that was a gift, our always too cold or too hot bathroom—form him, bring him into the world, and I hope it is okay. And how I too have been transformed by these actions, by the care that this ritual of bathing represents—made sensitive and percipient, covered, even, in a different flesh, it seems to me.

It is the repetition that gives this remembrance the feel of a haunting. Perhaps I used to outrun such hauntings by the inconsistency of my days, before I was slowed to our more bodily pace and repeating rhythms. I am more present in myself, and it turns out I am haunted.

From the irises I learn that my memories are out of time. I passed a clump in yellow flower, blooming in a front-garden, on our way to the disused nineteenth-century cemetery, where some days I walk and he invariably naps at my chest, in the city's answer to a forest.

I thought *how odd, they are late* because I saw irises rising out of the park-lake bloom and fade just a month ago.

Days later, as we walk our slow, sleeping walk past the park-lake this time, the irises growing there are in bloom too, of course.

It was not a month but a year ago.

The anaesthetist's eyes as he directed me to the plastic chair set against the side of the hospital trolley—I'm not sure if it was compassion I saw there, perhaps just tiredness; something solemn. I am not good at lying, but in that moment I feel the utter necessity of explaining out loud to my infant with full (and false) calm honesty that it is nap time and he will have a little sleep now as I hold him, facing out, against my torso and they place the small mask over his face. His trust in me and his fascination in this new place and people mean there is no struggle, and perhaps he is too young to register the crack in my voice. I feel his body soften in my arms. I don't recall if I laid him down or they took him from my lap. There is just a blind gap of memory, then I am broken down in the corridor, doubled over in breathless sobbing with the nurse standing by me, her hand on my back, waiting, I suppose, until I am consolable.

What if there is some danger in him? Something that will not be revealed until his precious skin is punctured. I could not bring myself to write in the few days before his minor-surgery but now, as he sleeps and breastfeeds and sleeps to recover, I can talk about this particular fear. I remember my ex's sister, as an adult, discovering an extra bone in her upper arm following an accident. And an anecdote recently shared about a head-injury revealing an especially large occipital lobe, revealing to the injured that her visual perception of the world was, and had always been, markedly different from most. Then there's me. I have hypermobility syndrome, or, more accurately I think, I am hypermobile. My tendons and ligaments, my veins, my responsiveness to pain killers and anaesthetics, my stomach (and more no doubt of which I am less chronically aware)

are, to a degree, ineffectual (of course it is the drugs that are ineffectual, but this is not the way I feel it). But I look fine, tired now, but fine, and went undiagnosed until the age of 31, despite (or I sometimes feel because of) 10 years of protestations that *something isn't right*, and indications (mainly pain) since childhood. So I am acutely alive to the possibility of passing for well, physically as well as mentally, when in fact something is awry.

I feel ashamed writing about my condition. I don't know why. Perhaps the years of being patronised, disbelieved and dismissed. Perhaps the self-preserving notion in many of *the well* that we choose to be sick (particularly the chronically so), that I must, somehow, be doing this to myself, and enjoying it.

When, finally, 10 years after an accident from which I never fully recovered, my diagnosis was confirmed, I was invited to an Information Session about my condition. What soon became apparent at this gathering of chronically ill women with the format of a corporate training afternoon was that, for many, it was not the condition itself that was traumatic (though it can be hellish when un-managed), it was the years of struggle to be believed that had altered us the most.

And then there is so much in motherhood that is hidden, so much waiting to be revealed, so many invisible processes that require so much faith. A faith that does not come easy (if at all) to me, as someone who wants to see in order to know.

I felt as if he might simply deflate when cut.

Aside from the scattering of bruises on his shins from fearless crawling and the temporary, often theatrical, maquillage of food applied to his face at each meal, he has rarely been marked.

Today he is peppered with signs of yesterday's surgery, each of which pulls low at my stomach as I notice them again and again through my daily interactions with his body.

In particular, the tiny bruise and red-brown pin-prick to the back of each of his hands and the marker pen arrow, black fading to blue, on his left thigh. Also, the unexplained bruise on his left cheek, two stitched incisions in his groin and grey, empty outlines from the heart monitors.

But no secret was revealed. He is recovering well.

It is summer again now.

The past two summers trouble me and press their presence against the green of parks and trees in the city.

A summer from 30 years ago pushes to the fore. Beside the Tarmac playground was a kind of walled lawn, unkempt and edged with plants that had stood their own against neglect. I sat in the corner furthest from the school building, beneath a thin cluster of apple trees, in grass so long a child (as I was) could feel hidden. Over the red-black brick wall was a narrow, old road and then a graveyard. I was fantasising about running away to the graveyard, which held the profoundest fascination for me. This fascination was so palpable I can still bring it into being, almost, though I find it impossible to name from the point of view of a child, when desire was not the same thing as it is to me now. The graveyard belonged to a part-medieval/part-19th century church and with the imaginative temporal flexibility of a child I could, by inhabiting that space, inhabit the past. And even another almost primordial time in the mulching ground the damp crawling nature softening stone.

I was exquisitely alone and happy in the long grass, beneath the trees.

Two summers ago I was pregnant. The mystery which he remains to me had barely begun its process of at once unraveling and forming; simultaneously revealing and obscuring itself as he comes ever further into the world. Debilitating nausea had, at this point, settled as a permanent state and would remain so for a full, not quite biblical, thirty days.

There are certain physical states, like pain or nausea, which by their nature are temporary, except not always, in fact often not. I should be used to this, and I guess I am, which is perhaps why this solid, intransigent nausea felt like a curse, or worse, an accusation.

When the expected temporal limits of sensations like pain or nausea are crossed one might expect the sensation itself to change—it's impossible, surely, to be in pain for fifteen years, to be on the point of vomiting for a month—but they change less than you might imagine.

Last summer I walked and walked and walked.

It is not even really summer yet. Just an unseasonably warm May. But it seems I no longer go by calendar-seasons, though I am ruled by my google-calendar-diary and would be lost without its reminders.

Today it is summer, tomorrow it might be spring again or even autumn if he needs a cardigan and his leg-warmers. I wonder if my perception of time was permanently altered by that strange otherness of the peculiar temporality of labour—when time was barely time but rather waves—and I have never had call to return to time as it was before. Not that I am stuck in labour's time but, rather, temporal options have perhaps been opened up by passing through labour's strangeness.

I was not expecting to still be writing about his birth here, but why not, I guess. Like these summers that have not stayed where I left them, his birth is, perhaps, one of my ghosts.

I am starting to see this writing as a way of fixing my maternal experience, of pinning at least some version of this down before it dissolves and I am left only knowing that these things happened but no longer containing how they feel. And perhaps not even knowing that they happened after all. And of course the writing is a way of coming to an understanding of my experience in the first place—like the imaging I wrote of earlier, but more formalised, more controlled, though also more exposed, more fragile and compromised by language, by being made external.

I am thankful for it, the writing. If I can fix some sense of this time, create and contain some version, then perhaps it will not add to the ghosting that comes with the degradation, the thinning and crumbling, of what is retained. Or perhaps something else is true. Perhaps I am holding on to something that should be allowed to pass, perhaps I am *creating* a ghost of sorts, in the sense of something held-back, pulled out of the motion of time.

Though I strive for accuracy, and more, when I look back at the text where it has settled over time, it has shifted. So perhaps it fulfils the claims I make for preventing haunting or creating ghosts in part only, because ultimately it is something new. I think of the process of ceramics—the final glaze firing transforms what has in the most part, until that point, been a close, physical relationship between material and hand, and gives you back something you could not possibly fully recognise, something you did not know you were making.

I did not realise the extent to which language was already functioning between us until I watched back a video taken on his first birthday.

Do you want some more cake?
Yep

I had not fully registered this development and so barely recognise the versions of us playing back over and over on my phone. This is a common enough relationship to recordings, but when I think of it in terms of this sense of haunting that has pervaded my experience of mothering it takes on a slightly altered light. What exists in the gap between my over-tired perceptions and other registers of experience, I find disturbing. Disturbing in being both present and absent, evidenced but unremembered—ghostly.

I had been meaning for weeks to take him to the V&A Museum, on some kind of odd pilgrimage to the object I had found, searching the online archives, resembling the vessel I pictured, so fully, breaking in my chest, leaching emotion and awakening ghosts. Illness, tiredness and difficult days had rolled this non-essential task over from week to week, but I decided finally to go. I checked the archive listing I had bookmarked for the object's location in the museum and already there was a slip—the accompanying photo had been updated from a suggestive, partial image, to a more explicit shot of the whole object, side on. It no longer suggested the vessel I had imagined, that I had seen and still see, lodged, broken behind my ribs.

Still, I was determined to seek it out—perhaps the resemblance suggested by the earlier photograph was still there, in the flesh, or perhaps I would find something else. And I had promised myself I would take him to play in the fountains of the museum's courtyard. As I struggled to contain his 14-month-old desire for constant movement and exploration on the tube journey from East to Southwest London I could feel in the gently pervading air of anxiety that I was too tired for this. But then we had made it, without tears and, through his impression of a tiny commuter, in his own seat, discarded newspaper in hand, had spread some bashful smiles.

The sixth floor of the V&A, where the object is apparently housed, was closed that morning, suddenly and temporarily. We wandered a little, drawn into the darkness of a small cinema space where a film about the Great Exhibition played to empty benches. Here he could crawl on the carpet and breastfeed a little in the dim space while narrators spoke the preserved letters of Great Exhibition visitors. There are so few spaces where his energies feel appropriate rather than disruptive. This domestic-sized and, importantly, empty cinema felt like a relief. And, purely for myself, I am closest to some kind of comfort in the dimmed, cheap-red-velvet spaces of cinemas and the cool of museums.

He was joyous in the fountains. I wrapped him in my scarf to keep the breeze from his damp body as he sat on the hand-towel I'd brought along and repeatedly lurched in an effort to return to the water. I felt self-conscious in struggling with what was clearly a two-person job, to dry him and re-dress him between the fountain and the inexplicably sodden grass I had planned to picnic on. So, lunch in the museum café, opposite a work meeting of well-dressed, handsome people, and between a tourist couple and a local grandmother who smiled and chatted a little.

Settled in his sling, his head folded to my chest in an overwhelming sleep barely out of the museum. He slept the journey home as I read on my phone over his shoulder. There was no object to speak of. Perhaps I was wrong to seek out the material counterpart to something hidden, haunting and imagined. I'm not sure now why I did—simple, casual intrigue or the desire to *see*, to be able (in theory of course) to hold?

I haven't written for a while, a few weeks I think. The light summer evenings seem to have inspired a shift in his rhythms towards a later bedtime so now we play when I used to write, and my thoughts are slow and heavy with tiredness by the time, finally, I feed him to sleep. Picturing all this, I realise there is a particular kind of play reserved for the end of the day— practical and focused, relaxed and independent, domestic. Emptying his drawers is a favourite. But I want to write and, thankfully, the nights are drawing his bedtime back from its solstice peak. So I begin again, in spite of the doubts, insecurity and exhaustion that have, all three, grown to fill the space.

I read back the last paragraphs I wrote, two or three months ago now, and barely remember having written them, at night no doubt, as I am now, poised to shut the iPad's cover should he stir beside me. Though things have changed, recently—his sleep has altered its nature, deepening and thickening so that he can no longer sense my absence through it, as he could, somehow, within two minutes of me leaving the bed—so I could write elsewhere tonight, but it's me that has to adjust now to this new-found freedom. So here I am, still, in the dark.

Superstition was a form of comfort as well as fear when I was a child—a way of systematising a seemingly unsafe and unstable world and forming controls (or obsessive behaviours, depending how you look at it).

And in the lack of control engendered by my experience of motherhood—my every action has to be negotiated with him, my financial independence has evaporated, I am at the mercy of sudden depressive or anxiety-laden patches of days, I rarely get to use the toilet alone, and so on—the pull, or perhaps presence, of superstition is strong.

I have a letter in my bag from the new NHS therapist, confirming to my GP her offer and my acceptance of a year of weekly sessions. She states, based on her assessment, that I use intellectualisation as my main defence in an attempt to control my emotional experience, "to the extent that [I make my] disturbance the object of [...] academic study". She goes on to suggest that I am likely to find the process of exploratory psychotherapy "challenging", though she thinks I will benefit from it.

I place my superstition and intellectualisation side by side—both, apparently, questionable as coping strategies.

I sit against the headboard feeding him, the top of his head nestled into the flesh of my arm and belly as he feeds. We fill the middle third of the mirror, side-on, recalling his birth in an unexpected wave of bodily memory. Though I never saw it in the small, round hand-mirror—which I insisted the midwife use to dispel her disbelief that he was there, crowning—in that state of labour I seemed to be seeing *with* my body and I could see the precise shape of the top of his head as my body rested a moment before another wave and he was out below the water.

So it seems I am still writing about his birth. That its ghost is still present enough to make itself known at the sight of the top of his head in the mirror. I feel wary of this, as if I might be open to accusations of obsessing about or dwelling upon it, of being disturbed by the power of the experience. As if anything above a certain register of affect is unacceptable, and time is perhaps one axis of the graph.

Here I feel a kinship to the ghosts of novels, who seem so often driven by a single-minded commitment to *feeling*, with as little thought for the proper limits of time as for the boundaries between living and dead. The ghostly-lovers of Virginia Woolf's short story, *A Haunted House*, whose faces *search the sleepers and seek their hidden joy* over centuries. The treasure they seek is, it seems to the haunted, *the light in the heart*, of lovers *sound asleep. Love upon their lips.*

Our communication is building to include overt signs and words, and though I hope this building is upon that other register of subtly reading one another—with various degrees of success and with a vertiginous feeling of transparency on my part—I wonder if some of that subtlety is already being lost to the expediency of language. Or confused by language's ability to dissimulate, perhaps. Or perhaps that's just my ambivalence towards language, and my sadness at the loss of a stage now coming to an end. I have, after all, begged for language as a *glorious, glimmering hope*, yet now I return to my familiar attitude of suspicion.

I remember the moment when I realised he and I had begun to have a history, and as such, it was possible for regret to begin to form. He was three months old and it was no longer *all to play for*, some of it was done. And whilst I didn't have regrets yet, not concrete ones in any case, I could imagine them forming, unseen, as our past gently piles up. Fed by the drip, drip, drip of guilt and uncertainty and shaped by the pressure of *making it up*, of trying to do it differently.

While I wait for my session I always sit in the same seat, by the part-open window that looks out over the patch of grass, trees and shrubs that constitutes the hospital grounds. The breeze on my neck feels like a counter to the subterranean sense, though we are on the first floor, of the endless corridors that make up my way to the therapist's office.

On the ground floor the corridors are that inexplicable whitish-red that somehow isn't pink, whilst upstairs they are relentlessly grey and sectioned by many doors like the regular divisions of an ammonite. Each week, the therapist leads me from the waiting room to her office, through a string of these doors, and as my muttered *thanks* peter out by the third door and I consider from behind what she's wearing this week, I wonder if she is angry with me, though I don't know why.

Last week a dray of baby squirrels played in the top of one of the trees outside the part-open window, amongst the blunt ends of branches that had been unceremoniously cut-back in full leaf. I watched them in wonder. They were not there this week.

Our weekly session has aligned itself roughly with the final 50
minutes of daylight, as we near winter and the days shrink,
so that the small window behind her seat, giving on to a roof
and a triangle of glass opposite, grows bluer throughout, and
sometimes burnt corals of sunset are visible.

I describe to her a dream I had recently. Describing the dream
I feel like a cliché of a therapist's patient. Or like a fraud, as if I
made it up to please or to test her. But I go on anyway. What's
strange about this dream is how little the central image has
faded, how clearly I can see it, still, some weeks later.

I'm on some kind of raft or inflatable, floating in the sea, near a
boat. There are other people in the water too and someone, a
woman, holds the edge of my raft and we chat. Then I notice,
right below us, beneath the water, three or four orcas, rolling
upwards and then plunging down without breaking the surface.
The smooth curves of their black backs pushing up the water
are breathtaking—I am both awed and terrified. Others in the
water begin to notice them and panic. I'm concerned that the
kicking legs of the woman I was speaking to, who is still holding
on to my raft, will get us both killed.

The strange combination of recognising him, or a likeness in him, often mine, and feeling him a stranger, not just unknown but unknowable—a different kind of consciousness—catches me at points throughout our weeks.

I'm struggling to recall a conversation with my brother—he was describing an hallucinogenic trip and it sounded so much how I imagine an infant's consciousness might be. Or rather, it was the first time I felt I could imagine such a thing. But I can't remember now what he said, only that the trees in the cemetery park were deeply green as we walked in the afternoon sun and I am still always surprised how tall he is.

This recognising/unfamiliarity is there between us too, my brother and I. It was always commented upon how unlike my parents and brother I looked—jokes about the milkman—but as we age and our bones make themselves more prominent under the softening fat of our faces, he and I begin to look more alike, though not really.

People tell me almost daily that my son looks like me, that he has my eyes. And sometimes I am spooked by the sensation of my own eyes looking at me from his small face. When I tell the therapist about this I'm keen to stress that I don't see it as a good or bad thing—I am not happy or unhappy that he resembles me—but it is unsettling.

It is so hard to separate out the many parts of this experience. Is it really his similarity to me, in temperament as well as looks, that causes me to question the nature of our separateness, or is it, rather, the fact that almost two years after his birth he is still such a long way from independence, from not needing another person to ensure his survival, let alone his flourishing? Winnicott's well-used idea that there is no such thing as a baby, only a baby-plus-carer, seems to me to hold largely true for a toddler too.

As I describe to the therapist feeling, sometimes, that I cannot really see him, I invoke him with a wave of my hand.

Sometimes when I hold him it's as if nothing is there. Like the opposite of a phantom limb, perhaps I feel him as a part of me and when I don't seem to exist the same, in that moment, goes for him?

I can see how exquisite he is, how exquisite this moment is but I seem to feel too little. I only notice this sometimes, though it is not always easy to place an absence.

As I cup his soft cheek in my hand, his face close to mine, I'm aware again that my hand seems not to belong to me. It's not hers this time, but nor is it mine. Stephen Frosh writes, *without recognition, we do not know if we are alive.*

The world shivered as I placed my glass on the kitchen worktop, as if with a small tremor, but it was a migraine just beginning.

I've never seen the scar where she slit her wrist. She wears a wide silver bracelet now which I assume conceals it.

Still, at twenty months, he sometimes wants to occupy that space he held before he was born. I lay on my side and he is curled up where my pregnant belly used to be, his feet and bum against my thighs, drawn up at a right angle from my hips, his head at my breast and his forearms against my ribs.

Though I remember him mostly the other way up, with his feet digging into my splayed rib cage and his head reliably on my bladder—so reliably that the trainee sonographer sighed in relief as the little head she was struggling to locate was indeed where I half-joked it would be, using my bladder as a pillow.

At a sudden noise, a door blowing shut in the flat or our neighbours greeting friends in the corridor in effusive Portuguese, I wait, like waiting for thunder after lightening as I was taught to do as a child, counting the seconds to calculate its distance.

I wait for him to stir, calculating how deeply he sleeps by the delay, the depth of sleep that the sound needs to penetrate.

One of my strongest memories of being pregnant, perhaps because it is a composite of a simple, repeated event, rather than a single instance, is of walking from King's Cross station to the office where I was working part of the week, in Bloomsbury. It's a ten-minute walk by the back streets. First past rows of small hotels, then courtyarded blocks of council flats punctuated by pubs. Some combination of the awareness of my altering body in motion and the sense of privacy in this small space of in-between time, made those minutes joyful—it was just us, together, walking.

And, as long as I avoided the butcher's shop, my nausea was eased slightly, or distracted from at least, by being in the open air. I listened to the birth playlist I'd been making, trying to imagine what music wouldn't annoy me during labour. In the end there was no space for sound at all in the internal world of my labouring. I made loud sounds, but it was, I think, more physical than oral, the sound-making. The sound was a by-product.

As I walked, I imagined my pleasure translating itself into his pleasure as he made first tiny bubbles of movement and later great wet sea-creature cartwheels.

Sara and I talked about loneliness in what felt like a breach of some social etiquette around the depth of conversation one can have in a crowded shopping centre on a Saturday afternoon, toddler in-tow. Earlier I had told her about another feeling—like grief or heartbreak or terror—like waking up knowing something terrible has happened but not remembering yet what it is. Only I never remember. The feeling is separate, self-sustaining it seems, uncoupled from any *thing*.

I think my anxiety creates a kind of drag to his crying too. Though it's usually brief really, these days, it continues, or its possibility does, within me for some time. It reminds me of paint dragged across canvas or of the way a single point touched to a pot being thrown on a wheel becomes a continuous line, encircling the pot.

Is it loneliness—this wanting something, but not knowing what that something is?

There was a certain necessary giving up I finally came to
practice when he was 18 months old. Life was too difficult,
and suddenly I saw clearly that I needed to give up all but the
essentials. I'm not sure I quite managed this. And after all, how
do we decide what is essential?—this writing could be the most
or least necessary thing. In any case, I acknowledged the quiet
state of emergency we were in, particularly with his father's
health and what that really meant, and still means, for how,
realistically, we might function.

When I look back, as I am writing this a little out of time, I
see it as a descending calm. It reminds me of walking home
through ancient streets covered in settled snow, quietened by its
blanketing white, yet made expansive by the simplicity of a single
blank surface.

Our circle of travel narrowed: if you want to see us you have to
come here. I know people don't understand, I fear I wouldn't
have. But I have seen the limit of my energies, and what lies
beyond, and I must stay within that limit—it is a hard limit, not
a warning.

In what Freud would term an *auditory hypnogogic hallucination*, his little sounds ring with an odd clarity in my head as I try to fall asleep. TA, TA, TA for water, CUCK a merging of duck and quack. They are crisp and whole, complete, in spite of their fragmentary or compound natures. The words *crystal clear* come to mind and I imagine, in my sleepy drifting, these crisp sounds existing in a hollow, crystal-walled space within my head—like one of those deep caves discovered now and then harbouring unclassified microbes at inhuman temperatures. The information of his sounds is surprisingly uncorrupted, unedited, by the process of memory. I have them complete, not partial or condensed—such is their importance.

I had another of my sea-life dreams, as I think of them, almost as if dreamt to order, to offer up to the therapist whose poker face betrays her when I talk about the dreams.

Last time it was black sharks with velvet skin, this time fish, rays, octopus, mostly at the bottom of a swimming pool. A girl dives in.

I saw his breath in the cold air as we waited to cross the main road, and had a sudden, new sense of his existence. The space of his little lungs pouring out in pale breath, this breath with which I have been so engaged, so vigilant of, suddenly visible.

In the moments after his birth I did not feel his presence quite as I felt I should—though he suckled, skin to skin, in my arms, on my chest. I still feel that way sometimes, that I cannot really experience his presence. I wonder though if it is an issue of distance, of separation. That just as he is still working on seeing me as someone separate, I am working on feeling him to be that too. My love for him is not that romantic love of longing, always somewhat unsettled by the negotiation of the many distances between at least two adults.

My love for him is fierce but almost invisible in its flooding of me. I have worried about this invisibility, without the friction *romantic love* uses to make itself visible. I worry too that because we are not quite separate, I may sometimes love him as I love myself.

Five days after his birth I began to cry uncontrollably with fear that he would cease to exist—was this what I had expected at his birth? My emotions rarely seem to me correctly calibrated—always too much or too little and often out of time.

I was nervous of being thrown together with other mothers, and the occasional father, imagining it might be a bit like school, all hierarchies and power-play. But it hasn't been that way for me, here. It has been a strange intersection with the lives of these other mothers with whom I share a sudden, patchy intimacy.

We sit on the library floor and talk about breasts and nausea and fear. Our children play together or cling to us. I know most of these women only barely, though some well, and our conversations are fragmented by the demands of our babies and children, but certain barriers are down. One of these women threw herself from her balcony, last week, I am told by another.

There was a day just before his second birthday when suddenly the light was completely different and it seemed winter had passed, as if all of a sudden. We spent the afternoon in the sandy play area of the park. The little clusters of faux boulders emerging from the sand gave long shadows in almost amber light. He worked, as toddlers so conscientiously do—his activity is usually more work-like than play-like in appearance, Maria Montessori would be unsurprised to observe—piling handfuls of sand onto the boulders, or rather onto a particular spot on a particular boulder that seemed to speak to him of needing to be piled, carefully, with sand. We were there again today, among the big, old trees of the park—a park originally built, my neighbour told me once, to keep the people of East London from cluttering up Regent's Park, to keep them in their place.

There was water in the sand today and it brought him such peace to stand in the water and gather handfuls of wet sand. I think so often of a line from Mary Oliver about how the trees save her (she would almost say) *and daily*. Ordinarily I prefer winter, but in this new life—where it seems his ideal is to spend most of the day outside, covering small distances slowly, handling the often damp world—winter feels like something we endured. Now we are free to play in the sand and grass, on the slide and swings, to quack at the ducks and throw stick after carefully chosen stick into their large pond, to stare at the iris roots visible beneath the water and the tiny insects skimming, to notice and name the moon in the afternoon sky and to chase other people's footballs.

Two strands of thought wove themselves together as
I wondered about the feeling, still present, that I am
experiencing the world now more as I did as a child. An obvious
explanation would be that I am reminded by his childhood of
mine, and that's a part no doubt, but that's not really it.

I've been reading a lot of D. H. Lawrence (although his writing
troubles me, it is available free on my phone and I cannot
afford my novel habit otherwise) and feeling some specific,
current resonance in his listy descriptions of nature. There
was a moment in my reading of *Lady Chatterley's Lover* where
the seasons fell into sync, and I recognised his list of blooming
plants as blooming here and now too. I had seen them all just
that day as we walked through the city park to the duck pond
and sandy play area. Though I wondered how much, in the
intervening 90 or so years, the changing climate has shifted that
particular season-within-a-season.

But I think it is the fact that since becoming a mother I
have spent so much of my time outside, roaming the parks,
playgrounds and cemeteries of East London, that brings
me back to some part of myself that was more to the fore in
childhood (despite the suburban nature of my own). I felt then
a profound connection to plants, trees in particular, sky, mud
and stones, and most profoundly the rain. As a small child I
would drag a stool out into the garden and sit, half sheltered by
the shallow eaves of a suburban newbuild, in the evening rain.

At 29 I read Steinbeck's *To a God Unknown*, and found there
some image of this profundity I had felt and lost touch with, and

was, particularly at that moment it seemed, yearning for. That book at that moment felt serendipitous and necessary, though I had stumbled upon it almost arbitrarily. I felt hobbled by circumstance and unable to act on this recognition, this lighting up in me of something old and precious. Then the summer passed and autumn quelled this risen need a little with its softer light and sheltering skies. I got caught in a rainstorm back where I come from, having visited Sara, walking for the train back to London. I was soaked through to my skin. That helped too.

So now I am crouched by the duck pond, holding his hood to make sure he doesn't fall in as he swipes the water with a long twig, or walking the stretch of canal from Fish Island to the Olympic Park to save bus fare, or following him steadily as he runs between raised flower beds in the magical little park nestled between tower-blocks, old and new, and motorway, ten minutes' walk from home. And that connectedness I spoke of is fed by this time amidst the grass, leaves and flowers, the trees shushing overhead or erupting in the sudden caws of crows. The sunlight on my skin.

His sleep-sweated head smells like things found in a rock-pool and left out to dry in the sun and breeze. Vegetal but also flesh and salt.

The trees are in full leaf now and I cannot see the place where the squirrels played. Though the bare stumps of heavy branches cut off still show themselves above the fall of leaves hanging from bended, lighter, newer shoots all about them.

In writing this I comfort myself in my waiting, nervously, to be called. Always nervous at being called. Though she doesn't really call me, just appears at the door with a withheld smile that indicates I must rise and follow her.

I stumble upon an image of a whale, while researching projects for my day-job that I mostly do at night while he sleeps. It was skimming the surface of the water from beneath, like the orcas of my dream. I had the same dread-fascination feeling across my skin, as if I had some real knowledge of the power there in that creature, as if I had a memory of it.

I must have watched her daily absence. This mistake between presence and absence—a presence that is in fact mainly an absence, or an absence the presence of which is felt—seems to me the definition of haunting.

I've never heard her laugh.

It's odd that I should write at all really, when, as the NHS therapist and I establish, I am unsure that I even exist. Am I trying to make myself a shadow, show myself that I *am* in the world, that I might be gently and insubstantially traced upon it in some shifting form.

I remembered Ruth's hands. She was a tutor on my first degree
—teaching the block of lectures on Byzantine Art. I wrote about
the iconoclasm and became briefly fascinated and perplexed
by the issue of representing gold—gold tesserae, gold paint—in
photographs, the photographs that illustrated my textbooks.
For gold seems to be a state of light in other ways than only
colour, and holds such extreme possibilities, such darkness and
brilliance.

She had the most beautiful hands. I noticed them early on
during the first lecture. They tapered to her fingertips, smooth
and a little too white, like the impossible bodies painted by
Ingres. She had been a biochemist, I think, but had given it
up to become an art-historian and it seemed to be making her
happy. I still see her beautiful hands, sorting notes at the front
of a bland, upstairs classroom.

Something in his consciousness has shifted and he is truly a little bit a stranger to me. And perhaps to himself too.

I feel it is so hard for them, the toddlers, such huge leaps, such straining at anchors and such revolutions.

Puts a finger to its lips or a hand over my mouth

It is a quiet, everyday madness.

I want to write something about how autumn has come and how he is obsessed with picking berries from the low bushes that edge the park. And how I'm struck for the first time by the beauty of these tiny multitudes—the green ones that turn slowly, over the weeks, a matt black, the ones that look like cherry-coloured glass with blushes of dense black and highlights of scarlet just beneath the surface, the coral ones that somehow I imagine I know from the Christmases of my great-grandmother's Edwardian childhood. Perhaps she picked them on her way home from the big house where she was a servant, for the brief holiday.

He calls them *bellies* and says the green ones are *tiny, tiny balloons*, which is exactly what they look like.

Impossibly old Bangladeshi women, who pass us as they walk in shuffling steps to sit in the city park or tend the small allotment beds opposite the berry bushes, smile at him with such intense longing it breaks my heart and I ask him if he'd like to say hello, which sometimes he does.

It still happens, quite often; I do not see my hands, holding or touching my child, as my own but, rather, as hers. And the churn of my stomach, then a brisk acceptance of this small catastrophe and a decision to go on, more saddened that frightened these days. Is that what happens, sometimes, when one becomes familiar with one's ghosts—fear turns mostly to sadness, and some anger.

I feel, alongside whatever prompted the gesture, apologetic when I touch him. When I stroke his hair across his warm forehead or place a settling hand on his stomach, feeling his lower ribs. As if reading my mind, he takes my hand and wraps it around his little foot.

When I think of the river it is low and muddy, weighing down the inverted spine of the urban valley in which I lived as a child.

It always felt like being in a valley, weighed down, the sky obscured and smaller than it should be.

But anyway.

He was calm on the bus today. I noticed his contentment to be in his pushchair and actively observe the passing world, not straining for movement as he so often is, buckling against the pushchair clips and almost tipping the thing over with the force of his small body. It is a relief, this calm, and I value it.

From the top of the playground slide he looks at the sky and we talk about how today it is white, *all white*. It gives an odd colourlessness to the air, with the faint drizzle that darkens the wooden structures he's climbing. *Black wood*, he says. *Black hair*, he said of the mould that dots our bathroom ceiling, breaking my heart.

Unlike the thronging summer days, the playground is almost empty. A little girl who refuses to wear a jacket or even a jumper and instead periodically re-warms herself by wrapping the coat her mother is wearing around herself too and clinging, head to one side, to her mother's breast. The scene reminds me of how I used to wear my son, as a baby, in his fabric wrap under my coat, pulled around us both as I walked and walked, in this same park. I have never felt a sense of geographical belonging but I start to think that all those circles I have walked around this large park have marked, like some slow rite, a sense of place that I might choose to call mine.

Slide, stones, swing, slide, stones, swing. With demands for singing, and faster, and quiet. Exerting the powers he is finding in language. And I am so thankful to be outside. Almost leaving as the rain grows heavier, but then it eases again and a reprieve, to stay in the open air, where we both so badly need to be. Eventually it is time to go: five minutes, one minute, now it's time.

That dream sense of something unexpected but also completely accepted, or at least already happening.

He bit me again and I held him away from me, gritting my teeth to keep the power from my hands around the small bones of his arms. As I placed a hand against his ribs to keep him away from pulling my hair I felt the rapid beat of his heart and suddenly what I knew was happening was no longer theoretical, it was embodied.

The struggle to hold, above the high-water mark of my anger, the knowledge that his actions aren't what they seem—he's desperate and has lost control, though it just looks like he's enjoying hurting me. But his heartbeat brought me back to our bodies.

I look away from what I'm reading on my phone for a moment, to see his face. He's asleep at my breast, and he looks exactly as he did in those first few days—one hand curled around the breast, a knuckle of the index finger resting on his nose, the other hand with fingers gently curled, resting on his cheek, making a slight impression in the soft fat of his face.

It is a wordless love, outside of language.

The strip of light from between the edge of the ill-fitting blackout blind and the window frame creates an out-of-focus camera obscura on the wall and I watch the cars and lorries flow along the A12. Blurred rectangles but discernible in their smooth, paced, two-way flow. Sized like his toy trucks.

I think about staring at walls from a bed. I think about Charlotte Perkins Gilman's short story *The Yellow Wallpaper*, where postnatal depression becomes, in the crucible of medicalised incarceration, psychosis. Specifically the protagonist is kept from writing.

The space felt like a stage in a way, all curtains, no real walls, dimly lit. A stage before the curtain's up. I apologised for bleeding on the floor and the sonographer was endlessly kind. It would take my body longer to realise I was no longer pregnant, and the nausea, with which I was to become so familiar, next time, remained a while. This happened a long time ago now.

When I name it—broken-hearted—it is like centring clay on a wheel, a sudden stillness, full with movement, and I can see its dark centre for a moment.

She also, I was told, hacked her wedding ring in half with an axe. I have known this for years now and still don't know what to do with it.

He has dropped his nap and so the weight of the work shifts, from two distinct sections punctuated by a stillness of sleep to one unbroken day. The day is shorter overall as he goes to bed earlier and easier now, but I am finding it a struggle to adjust how I manage my stamina over this unbroken stretch. I don't remember how long it is now that he has been napping once a day (before that it was twice, earlier still it was three times and in the beginning it was uncounted), but it seemed like an unshakeable routine, and yet, simply overnight, it stopped. His choice entirely.

As I walk home without him from the nursery and the low winter sun flashes in my eyes between railings, I feel that drag in my stomach that almost doubles me over, like a tightening of the diaphragm at the start of a panic attack. At once the loss of him, for a few hours only, and the in-flood of exhaustion and pain now that his need and distraction is absent.

Just as I am continually explaining to him why we must or mustn't do or go—with best results when I engage him face-on and little effect when I raise my voice from behind the pushchair or across the room—I am internally explaining to myself why it's ok really, though it doesn't feel ok, that it isn't real, I am safe, though I don't feel safe, and I am in control, though barely.

In the next-door café after our hour at the trampoline park—
where he had jumped, countless times, with sheer abandon from
the high bar into the adult-sized ball pit and bounded across
the grid of trampolines set into the floor, pausing only now and
then to gaze at the roving, coloured lights or demand I sing—as
our toddlers climbed to the highest point they could find, a
corner space behind the back of padded seating that ran along
the café walls, just as keen to test the limits of this space as of the
trampoline park, and we ate the food we had ordered for them,
Livi described to me the bad trip that had removed, momentarily,
her relation to reality and had taken her two years to recover
from.

Breathing snow onto the roof of my mouth.

There is snow this week and he is enthralled but not amazed. Perhaps he thinks *well, why not, anything can happen here.*

As we pass under a railway bridge on the way to nursery, we are momentarily both inside and outside the snow. It falls in front and behind, but we are sheltered in a space made suddenly empty by the fullness of the snow.

He sleeps, head against the pushchair's hood, *cave* he calls it. I slip off his snow-toed wellies and, as his blanket doesn't reach over his feet, take off my scarf and lay it over his mis-matched socks.

Like this he sleeps in the small hallway of our flat, next to the boiler cupboard. And I will check on him every few minutes until I hear him stir, wait, do nothing if he doesn't stir a second time or go to meet his waking gaze if the stirring continues.

I had another sea-life dream. Mostly I couldn't see the creatures clearly, though I knew what they were from their bloated shadow shapes and the way they moved in the water. It was a dream within a dream. I was pulled out to sea, a sea full of the terrifying masses of rolling sharks. I began to scream, and this scream became a panic attack, at which I became aware that the sea was a dream. Only later, when I woke, did I discover that the panic attack too was a dream. I had dreamed of dreaming about sharks.

I miss having a therapist to gift these dreams to. So here you go.

He is three now. He kisses the things he loves with little popping kisses.

I shouted at him in the forest and now he says *forest angry* as though the whole forest were angry.

I watch two small objects caught by the glance of light from beneath the door. I can't work out what they could possibly be.

They are both a similar size, that of a medium-sized pebble, and appear pale, possibly white. The one closest to the door appears to have a flat surface at a gently sloping angle, with a shallow-curved underside. The one a few inches to its left might have a convex surface or possibly be curved all the way around. Their lit profiles are reflected slightly in the dark grey of the painted floor.

The light coming under the door softens as it begins to rain outside—I can hear it through the window behind me, behind the blackout blind.

Most of his small objects are wooden or plastic, but these appear to be something else. He is drifting into sleep at my breast now, the movements of his arms becoming slower and the tension leaving his back. When he is fully asleep I can go and pick up the objects, but for now I just stare, affecting patience that is unnatural to me, and write this of course, one-handed on my phone. Eventually I lay him on the bed and cover his bare legs with a blanket, edge myself out of the bed and leave a roll of duvet in my place, between him and the edge.

I had forgotten about the objects but go back a few minutes later to see what they are.

A small piece of yellow pavement chalk broken in half.

The winter has been hard again. The indoor textures of carpet, padded plastic, hard plastic, vinyl and polished wood. When we are able to be outside, the grass or sand is a glory.

He asks me what they are as he picks up open handfuls of amber-brown fluff caught by the ridge of an uneven seam between concrete and grass. *Seeds,* I tell him, *from the trees.* I don't know the name of the tree that makes these multitudes of furry seeds that the wind blows, again, from his open palm.

And later we witness the moment a gust of wind pulls furls of petals from a blossom covered tree and fills the air with their suspended paper-snow bodies.

At the public swimming baths his brief caution quickly softened to intrigue and finally abandon as he tried to avoid the outstretched arms and jump into the water without being caught—he is aware of consequences, he understands I catch him for a reason, but he needs to take the chance anyway. He makes do with being caught, again and again, as he jumps from the matte-black ridged edge of the shallow kids' pool. And with my hand under his chest he, instinctively I think, begins to paddle his feet and we cheer in shared delight. Eventually we get out and when he realises there is no return from the grey damp changing rooms he cries inconsolably and begs to go back to the water. He is hungry and exhausted and I can almost see the new neural connections forming as he consolidates this new, watery experience.

And now it seems like it must have been days ago, but it was only yesterday—the event seems so significant it cannot possibly be so recent, it must, in a way, always have already happened.

The flanks of my lower back ache with either tiredness or sickness and as I pull his duvet a little further up over his torso I can feel the warmth of its underside where it has lain against him, holding his heat.

I fold myself in my own duvet next to him, feeling its coolness turn to warmth and shifting my legs to find new cool patches. He has seemed a little under the weather the past two days, asking to feed and seeming a little angry. I ache now and the back of my nose fizzes gently, suggesting I too am under the weather.

As I knelt in the long grass, which seemed determined to reach the height of the daffodil stalks weighted by their heavy, succulent looking seed heads, their blooming over, and I helped him in his search for dandelion *clocks* to shake, releasing snow-bursts of tufted white seeds, I thought about how I might write this and tried to name the smell of the grass/earth/buttercups/clover/daffodil stalks/bees/dragonflies and dandelions. It proved, in that moment, unnameable.

As he picked another dandelion head, he exclaimed triumphantly that the seeds had *come back,* performing a trick of imagination that stitched time back on itself so that this wasn't a new dandelion but the one he'd just *vooshed* returned to itself, made whole again.

For even this act of dandelion shaking has its violence within its joy, which he plays at imagining reversible.

He doesn't use speech factually but as a kind of representation or performance of feeling, variously abstract.

I was thinking about wanting to write something of his sleep. Drowsy with over an hour of breastfeeding, punctuated by his attempts to reignite the day and to resist sleep's seemingly insipid pull, I stumble to get the iPad for its white noise app (tried in one of many attempts to improve his sleep, but only effective on me) when the sky lights up a long moment.

Our seventh-floor corner flat affords large-sky views southwards and east. I turn off the lamp to remove the reflections from the glass, so only the beneath-glow of inner-city light dims the lightning a little, and I stand and watch. The thunder is so near constant that it sounds more like a gale blowing. My vision is quite migrainous today, as though my eyes are filmed with a kind of dirty gel, through which I watch the clouds glow with lightning.

I'm haunted by the words of Graham Swift's novel, *Mothering Sunday—She had not known he was already dead*. Every time my memory pulls them up, unbidden, and turns them over to examine, I shiver inwardly and feel a heat behind my eyes.

Books slip away as I read them, becoming a kind of aerated, holey, brittle substance, and settling as wordless ashes.

She told me on the phone that she'd been in the hospital because she had hurt her wrist. I don't remember when it dawned on me that she had tried to kill herself.

I offer up my wrists to the breeze, cool in the crooks of my downturned elbows, sun-warmth.

Sometimes I offer him roses to smell and he comes close and snorts into them in an estimation of sniffing not yet mastered.

We made, in a kind of controlled explosion of oats and sugar, flapjacks the other day, and when I ask what he put in them he always remembers only cinnamon and vanilla.

Several afternoons this week we've been to the splash-pools in the large park. They are formed of a snaking brick structure, like an earthwork in form but with channels of textured concrete punctuated by low fountains. Today, again, the drainage wasn't working properly and the pooling water was cloudy with toddler urine warmed by the sun. I think of Janet Frame contrasting the *honest* smell of infant urine with the smell of adults soaking in their own waste in the psychiatric institutions of her novel *Faces in the Water*. In the open air though, amidst the trees, there is no smell of urine, just of sun cream and warmed, sometimes perfumed, skin.

The energy of children in water is something I can barely begin to formulate. Some study the water's properties—how the fountains can be redirected with a well-placed foot, how their buckets fill and empty, how their toys react to this seemingly new element, what toys of others might be found floating, momentarily unclaimed, and explored. Others relate more architecturally to the surroundings, testing the sheerness of brick slopes and running the snaking course of the ever flowing mini-river, from the low flat-topped hill down to the gathering, shallow pool. He does all these things, one after another, sometimes finding a kind of reverie and spending whole minutes together filling a new bucket (the newness is important) from a spurting fountain. Or he will befriend a baby, bending down and tilting up his head to make eye contact, and ask them a series of unanswerable questions about themselves, then turning to me to ask the same questions in the face of the infant's lack of speech and my apparently omnipotent knowledge.

The area is exposed and there is little shelter. On the slightly cooler days, earlier in the week, there were only a few other people, but our last two visits have been at busy, frenetic times. I wade in the water too, unlike most of the parents who, depending on the independence or liability of their child, either stand at the edge or sit a little way off on the grass or benches.

The water is cool and moving across my feet and the rough, sand-coloured concrete gently scratches as I walk. He plays a mermaid, laying on his belly in the cloudy pool that just about covers the depth of his outstretched chest. I chat with a mother of a baby he has befriended and though she is lovely and I seem to enjoy and be engaged in our conversation, it is in fact like a small but panicking alarm going off inside my head, as almost all social interactions are. They leave before us as the baby needs a nap and we wave goodbye fondly.

Eventually, after an hour, maybe more, in the water—time too seems to be on a strange slow-draining and filling loop while we are here in the full glare of the early afternoon sun—it is time to go and I coax him over to the pushchair. I stand him on the wooden bench beside the pushchair and strip him of his wet swim clothes, wrapping his skinny, cold body in my oversized shirt in place of a towel while I gather his dry clothes to re-dress him. He is hungry after the water and we eat snacks as we head home through the park, streets, market, side streets and our own upwards-sloping street, always a last, tiring push on our return.

As my hands wrestle gently with his slow-flailing arms, only half controlled in his still-asleep, yet bolt-upright state and I smooth his body back down, like pulling at clay, to the mattress, I wonder *whose small arms are these?* as if, in the dark, I cannot name him. But the shock of the question brings me into myself and as I rest my hands over his right arm, securing his body back into sleep, I answer the question *his of course* and feel happy that I can, with some effort, recognise his skin and mine.

I want so much to write, but I am too tired.

The same is true tonight but, regardless, I sift through to see if there is anything that wants to be written.

From the window—the cool gilding of the tower blocks by the setting summer sun, and the train tracks appearing to emanate from just beside our block, snaking between everlasting construction works and on through the reflective buildings.

Back in the artificially dark bedroom after loading the washing machine, pausing, confused by the familiar controls, gathering the necessary command from somewhere and setting the machine going, glancing at the view on my way out of the kitchen-living room, I wrote the view east.

After the semi-transparent roof of the bus garage—*where the buses sleep*, I say to him, and where at night their lights make the roof glow a moving pattern of peach, yellow and red, as if some giant shimmering cuttlefish were slowly exploring the brick and glass tank—the view south begins with a bank of trees where the playground is. In summer these trees function a little like a sundial as a sharp seam of shadow and sunshine moves up their bodies, the blue-green shadow making the yellow-green sunlit leaves heartbreaking.

Suddenly I was confused by the small, crisp leaves blowing from the line of trees outside the museum, for it is early summer. Until I placed their paleness and shimmer-spinning as sycamore seeds.

I had been reading Janet Frame the night before, writing of sycamores in her childhood, in a short story called *Gavin Highly*—their seeds' ready falling seeming to her to be the event of the day.

We have all been sick and I have lost hold of time, convinced over and over again it's the weekend, though it's obviously Wednesday. Now it's Friday and the sickness is something I have traveled through and been changed by. Which seems ridiculous as it was only a vomiting bug. But it took such effort to go on looking after him once he was recovered and buzzing with his usual fury of energy and I was sweating and nauseous and dizzy. And it reminded me of pregnancy, and the thought of months like this was more than I could comprehend, even having experienced it, leaving me feeling frightened for my once-self and shaken by the parts I did remember.

Should I write about how he has discovered humour in the sounds of language—picking up on a word I stumble over, how funny the mangled version is. Repeating it for days to himself and to me, and laughing at the strangeness of its shape, knowing already that there is a pattern, and that this error-word does not fit. And now making up error-words of his own— *splargle!*—working so hard to formulate them in his mind, then offering them up with peals of laughter and an almost crazed joy in his eyes.

I feel at these moments that he understands language better than I, that he can see its very glowing core, its fibrous roots. Not only can he use it, but he can also play with it, affect himself with it. When I write, I feel that I am within sensing distance, just barely, of language's vibrating core, its power—but he is right at the centre.

The crows with their beaks open.

I've never seen them like that before, as they walk their rocking or hopping walks over the expanse of grass in the large park. Their heads are still, not bobbing like panting dogs, but I assume it serves the same purpose, that their open beaks cool them, if making them a little less dignified.

And while their beaks look tongueless, dark, hard and sharp-edged like emptied mussel shells, their boned tongues must be resting inside, for bird tongues have bones.

Each crow has its large, dark beak open as we walk past, sweating despite our summer clothes and feeling the absence of green in the expanse of grass, now turned a dusty old-paper colour.

We were just leaving the splash-pools, in the centre of the big park's east side, when the weather broke. He asked what the sky was getting and I replied *dark, it's going to rain*, then lightning forked across our view of the broad sky and I squealed at the sound of thunder close in the open.

He laughed at my reaction, not scared himself, but with the small look of questioning he has when he is checking I am just playing or excited, not scared. And I laugh and tell him it's only lightning and thunder and it's exciting. I cannot tell if he agrees, but he is interested in the sudden change of light, the blue-grey seeming to appear almost instantaneously, complete, though it must have drifted over as it is the light through rain clouds.

I hurry, a little nervous of the exposed park and its trees, towards the gate and the city buildings that do not look as if they are poised calmly with up-turned palms waiting to be struck by lightning, as the trees do.

Aya writes that she is *often still lost for words on how complicated a woman's life is*. I reply to say how true I think that is, and how it's only since having my son that I have started to be aware of many of the structures that make it so.

Last time we met, she told me how she had cried for her own mother that week, wanting to be held in turn as she held her son.

Reading a bookseller's description of *The Waves*, it sounded like the most beautiful book I could imagine.

I loved the book when I read it, but I still hold that other version too, the unread, described one, like a treasure.

In the psychologist's office, as she evaded my questions about my son's behaviour, his sometimes overwhelming responses to others' emotions, I wondered about the curtain behind her. It covered, judging by its proportions, a wide but shallow window in an internal wall at roughly chest height. It was an observation window, through which you might be watched, playing with your child.

The curtain reminded me of the decor of caravans, the kind we holidayed in in the 1980s—like the time we went to Scotland and I was plagued with a recurring dream that my eyes fell out, or when we stopped for a night at a disused-race-track-turned-caravan-park, and my brother and I ran, high up along the stalls, the smell of concrete and metal and grass. The strange scale of the curtain, wide and short, and its oddness in the middle of an internal wall, not coming close to ceiling or floor, was exactly like something you'd find in a caravan, perhaps concealing a pull-out table or a bed.

I managed not to cry at this visit, but then I didn't have to talk about my husband's health as he was present this time and it was not mentioned. But still, the absence, again, of an answer to my direct question—in essence *should we be concerned?*—was maddening. As was the suggestion that I am perhaps too attentive to my child's needs (as of course the problem always lies in the mother). As was the feeling that the ugly ruched curtain concealed doctors. Presumably not at this moment, but that kind of intrusion, being watched, leaves its mark on the architecture that facilitates it.

Someone has ordered the wrong sand, perhaps. Before long the pure orange will be blended with the great mass of rainbow flecked paler sand, but for now it sits in patches at spots around the sandy playground—something like a sea-less beach stranded in the middle of a city park. This unintentionally obvious renewal of the sand—replacing, presumably, all that carried away in shoes and hair, gritting the bottom of bags and wet clothes—seems to mark the end of the summer, like cleaning something before packing it away. But the sandy playground is still ours. Rather than the school holiday throngs there are just a handful of children on this windy, cool afternoon.

I am struggling without the valve of my work mornings as we wait in a transitional space between finishing nursery and starting pre-school. It's only a matter of weeks but without that quiet, focused, busy time, alone, I am falling apart. I can feel that I'm not holding my face in a suitably human and ok expression as I sit in the sand at the bottom of the big slide while he climbs the stairs again for another go. I am too slow to respond appropriately to others' attempts at conversation, not filtering and falsifying my response quickly enough to, in fact, respond. So I am relying heavily on nervous laughter in place of words, and sometimes just silence. Often the words are assembled in my head but can't seem to find their way out, subject to some kind of inertia or paralysis.

Rebecca only identified the blissful fullness that she had often dreamt, against the roof of her mouth, after she herself began to breastfeed her first child.

So much of this has been written in the soft referred warmth of our bed, in pitch dark or dim light. But now I'm in a café, having left him at his new pre-school for the first time, where he is completely overwhelmed. Last week I stayed with him, but now we need to begin to test being there without me, with so many other children in the space, and staff ratios that do not reflect his particular needs as (I will come to know for a fact) a neurodivergent child.

The school talks a good talk about supporting his needs, but ultimately the situation in itself feels untenable. I've been round and round in circles trying to invoke some other magically ideal option, but there has only been silence in return.

When he was a year old, and his child minder of a few weeks told me it wasn't working, even just two mornings a week— that she couldn't manage his bottomless emotions and his unyielding persistence—I didn't so much invoke as invent a better option, an option for him. Instead of returning to work as planned, I lived off credit cards for a year. In that year he spent one morning a week with Eve, his soulmate of a nanny and my only respite from 24 hour caring. In those mornings I cleaned or did freelance work or worked on my PhD proposal or a piece of writing which had been accepted for a book. Most of these things I did at night too, but sometimes the concentration of daylight, of morning, was necessary.

When he was just over two my credit ran out and Eve moved back to Australia so I tried, with much trepidation, a council run nursery, still just a couple of mornings a week, to cover the time I needed on top of evenings for freelance work. He settled well and the staff supported his needs and recognised our concerns, but the ratio of adults to children was twice what it is at pre-school.

Tonight, for the first time in three years and nine months I tell him I won't breastfeed him to sleep. He accepts this unilateral decision with little resistance, and I am relieved that perhaps this means he too is ready. When he eventually falls asleep— unable, without the usual signals, to easily locate the stillness he needs to allow sleep to overcome him—I am fine.

Until, later, I lay down to sleep and I begin to cry.

I have cried for four nights now, a feeling of loss and desolation appearing suddenly when all is quiet and I lay down to sleep. I had developed breastfeeding aversion and had to stop because of the overwhelming aversion (I can find no better word) I suddenly began to feel every time I fed him. I thought this ending would naturally preclude me from grief—relief saturating instead—but apparently not. I have no conscious thoughts of loss or *the end of something*, but I am, it seems, a little devastated.

We dropped, or the graveyard rose, so the train window was no longer eye level with the headstones but, rather, I was looking up at their bodies against the white sky.

Do you remember, that conversation in the corner of a dank East London pub? I was sober and you were quite drunk, so perhaps you don't. You told me how you had always felt, somehow, like you were not the first child, like some wonder or magic charge that should have glowed between your mother and you simply was not there. You just felt some part of the story didn't fit.

As it turned out, you were right. Your mother had another child before you, a child that was adopted out of the family because she was unmarried and those were the times. I think it was your father's child too, but I'm not sure of that detail. As an adult, the adopted child found your family and you met once or twice. Was that when you found out? I don't remember.

As we sat in the pub, probably a decade ago now, I tried to imagine how this sense of not being the first born had communicated itself to you, and to imagine your mother's experience, which are both, of course, impossible tasks. I thought about your story a lot while I was pregnant, and since. I make no claims to understand your mother's experience, but I do keep getting caught up in the sense of how physically I have been changed by pregnancy and birth, and how, in her situation, no matter how thoroughly I tried to bury my secrets, I would be stuck feeling this altered body unearthing them every time I moved.

His sleep-breathing is still so slight and near-silent at times that I am relieved to lay beside him, close enough to hear it in my sleep. At bedtime he played at being a baby, allowing himself to be held in that two-armed cradling manner, and then suddenly asserting himself a *big boy*, as if, each time, the transition had just happened, that very second.

As he sleeps now, legs tucked up and hands to face, his mass of curly hair hidden by the darkness and just the curve of his cheek with a little pale light, he is a baby and I find his sleeping babyness hard to reconcile with the ferocity of his waking energy and with his command of language that catches me by surprise, offering glimpses of his complex and unknowable inner life.

I wrote once of the mystery that he is to me at once unfolding and concealing itself. This continues to be true.

The ammonite walled up its previous homes as it outgrew them, though a tube (a siphuncle) extended through them from the animal's body and these disused chambers could be flooded or emptied to enable the ammonite to alter its buoyancy, to move.

Too-narrow corridors again, and muttered thanks. But this time it is not the semi-domestic space of the NHS therapist's office—lamp, cheap framed prints, the smell of stewing herbal tea—but an almost completely absent space with windowless walls the white of nothingness, so that the desk, empty but for a computer and unopened box of tissues, stands alien and strangely solid against a non-wall. It is a science fiction space of alienation and waiting. But the doctor and psychologist are polite and even a little warm, as if they don't realise we have walked into a space the walls of which might at any moment become infinite or absent or a forest, because this can't possibly be a real space where people work, assess and are assessed, it is too overwhelmingly unmarked, frighteningly inhuman.

On a side street, finding my way here, I passed the open back entrance to a floristry school. That green and yellow smell by the huge warehouse shutters rolled up loudly to reveal the cool flora-filled space, its enormous containers of oversized fronds and plastic boxes of floristry paraphernalia packing the dim double-height and somewhat belying the refinement of the East-London-posh flower shop that faced the main street.

Following my assessment I am still answerless, another two appointments are apparently necessary for other parts of the assessment process. Somewhat shaken and frustrated I do not walk past the florist school again but take the most direct route to the tube station, seemingly unable to gift myself that green and yellow smell and its attendant joy.

From the bridge over the canal he dropped brown leaves that he chose, each with frantic excitement, gifting them to wind and gravity to argue over on their convoluted descent to the water, drawing his arm back through the space between black, thickly painted, metal uprights to begin the process again. Dusk wasn't even imminent, but the low cloud gave a light that seemed to say at any moment one might look up and realise that night had fallen.

I was tearful and exhausted from some earlier marital conflict that had seemed to overturn all the coping and managing and endless accommodations to expose the rawness beneath these things. I was unsure if the rawness was the body of those things, its vulnerable parts suddenly turned to the light, or the rub of those things wearing away my skin.

My throat thick, I said it was time to go and cajoled him into his pushchair with promises of watermelon at the supermarket.

In the park, I'm in an old and new time both.

There is no sure footing here, and I realise that each new stage is haunted by one, perhaps several, now past.

In a small office-like space she started by saying there'd been a miscommunication and today I was not going to receive feedback from the previous three assessments, as their letter had stated, but, rather, she needed to ask me some more questions, because it wasn't adding up.

Head in hands, I groaned a small noise then sat back and looked at her. Though I clearly displayed many autistic traits, she explained, I did not fulfil one crucial aspect of the DSM 5 diagnostic criteria—something about communication, I'm still not clear what. But she had an idea something else might be going on and that was what the extra questions were intended to settle.

A little bewildered and angry, and slightly nauseous, I noted her effusive nods and knowing smiles each time one of my answers rang with her theory of why I find it so hard to be in the world, especially with other people. I mentioned OCD and she nodded and smiled a *see, you got there by yourself!* smile. Later, so I could recall it and know exactly what had happened, not just some muddle of inferences, nods and smiles, I stopped her: *So let me just get this straight, you're diagnosing me with OCD right? Yes*, she answered, smiling and with a decisive nod.

I don't deny this diagnosis, but it is not the whole story. It is the shadow of the whole story, of the fact that we should not be using diagnostic systems based on (male) children to assess grown non-male adults (I will, later, watch my own child assessed with the same materials), of the fact that OCD is a common misdiagnosis of autism, of the fact that one cannot unmask at will after 38 years.

He is sick again, with a fever and a retching cough. He's four now, but I sing him to sleep as if he were a newborn. He sleeps with his head on my stomach, one shoulder on my pubic bone the other on my thigh, his feet touching mine, exactly where he put himself for the comfort he needs in his sickness. Soon I'll have to move him awkwardly to the cool pillow that he chose tonight to forgo in favour of my soft stomach.

When I held him as a tiny infant, my body, I was told, would change its temperature to regulate his. I mourn, suddenly, the loss of such magical powers and the distance that replaces them. Though, as I place my palm against his forehead, I notice that his fever has dropped, and I laugh at myself for wondering if perhaps I still possess them.

Sara said my name and I knew someone had died. Kaye was one of my first crushes. Pale and full, with light in her eyes. Dying her hair red on a school trip to Norfolk. Later, with the opposite of fullness and with the light in her eyes blinding to look at. And I was always only on the periphery anyway.

Now my bones feel chilled, as though I have stood somewhere cold too long, completely still. Sara says it feels like one of us didn't make it.

I bend my knees, sliding to bring my hair beneath the shallow bath water. The resonance of pipes and my own body's sounds through the water's density coalesce into an imitation, imagined or real, I'm not sure, of my son's small voice. Just a sound of his, and I know it isn't really him as he is sound asleep in the next room, but I lift my head and wait, still and silent, just in case.

The dark or amber polished wood and the old-wool smell of the crewelwork kneelers, waiting for choir practice in the cathedral—I was alive in the feel of the damply-cool stone, through the soles of my school shoes and against my fingertips. Sometimes, too, I went to the cathedral alone, after school, to look at the votive flames and for relief from the uncomfortable, insubstantial, peopled present—its anchoring stone and warm wood. I had learnt little about ghosts then.

Now, something about the feeling of my voice singing, as I coax him into sleep, my eyes closed, my palm resting on his side, brings me back to the cathedral, to half-singing, as I was never very good, in the tiered choir stands.

The cathedral made the town a city, I was told, but this always seemed a technicality, the town being so un-city-like, so quaint with an edge of poverty threatening the veneer. That valley sense of running alongside a riverbed that made everything feel a little buried too, so the cathedral never seemed so bold as to stand out. Even the ruined castle on its low hill seemed like a souvenir of itself, sinking into its own moat.

But, of course, my vision then was coloured by a suffocating familiarity and my vision now by a horror at the vulnerability of my youth. The votive flames and the damply-cool stone were part of a longing for some gesture or some certainty that might ward off anxiety. I had not yet realised it came from within, perhaps not always, but already.

I would breathe deeply as I passed the iron fence dividing the cathedral's courtyard from a side street, making the most of the yellow roses spilling through in their perfect scent.

The calm of my voice now, a calm so well used it has become almost real (until, sometimes, it cracks under the pressure), the calm suggests a different set of circumstances, like some strange dubbing effect.

I could write about the sea. How this time we didn't go to the sea, though Adam drove us past the estuary, all mud at low tide, on the way to meet Beth and Theo at the house. And again at high tide, on the way back to the station, so the mudflats were soaked over and the water shone silver.

This time we walked inland instead, through meadows of thick grass and into woodland. Adam had to gently trick him into coming down from the ancient tree where he had decided he would like to live. Its thick, low trunk gave way to a kind of plateau at its centre, low, thick branches extending out from its edges. The plaited roots at the place most suited to climbing had taken on the dark polished look of oil-coated metal. Part of the tree had been burned recently and I felt ashamed, though the vandalism wasn't mine. I felt that the tree was weary and wanted to be left alone to feel the cold breeze and the damp ground.

In one of the meadows, he sat down in the deep grass and took to moving handfuls of perfectly mole-sifted soil from their tiny hill to form another. We joked about the mirage-like stately home that marked out its own incongruous brick rectangle amidst the green. The scent from the malt factory was everywhere.

He seemed tired from the travel and excitement of visiting friends, though it turned out he was coming down with chickenpox, the first visible signs of which blossomed the following morning on his neck and flanks.

So, the next day he and I spent at home, back in the city, forming an inventory of his growing number of spots, and thinking, intermittently, about the weary tree and the perfect grains of soil. As he checked my arm for chickenpox, I wondered whether the confusion between where my body ends and his begins works both ways.

He asks if his dad is nocturnal and I say *no darling, he is unwell remember, daddy is unwell, that's why he sleeps a lot.*

For the first few moments as we enter the cemetery park, its small forest space filled with broken-down graves, I am overcome by the early summer beauty of the place in wild leaf and flower. But the sterility of my suburban upbringing is outraged, and unease sets in as he lifts softly loose bark from a fallen tree, and I try not to think about the chaos of light-shy creatures dislodged. There is a buzzing too, some kind of hover-flies having their no doubt brief moment. Once I have heard it I keep hearing it, but it's the kind of sound you cannot distinguish as really there or an echo of your own disquiet.

We head a little way into the interior of the park and he says he is not sure he wants to come back here again *because it is dark*. But we find a sunlit clearing and he is happier there, throwing a ball up into the arms of a tree, his pushchair parked up and abandoned for now. Then he gains a little bravery and begins to explore beneath a low canopy of young oak and holly, ivy spread across the floor. He moves a little way from me and says I must find him, turning his nervousness, at the wildness of the place, into a game. He is never out of sight and barely out of touching distance, but if I pretend, with exaggerated gestures, that I cannot find him for longer than he has silently prescribed he says *I am here*.

Then, as he crouches by a row of headstones that seem as much to emerge from as to sink into the foliage, he asks who is that on the pushchair? I look back and say, laughing, that it is only his sun hat resting there, but I am shaken and want to leave. He looks, his head tilted, and repeats his question, I give the same answer and suggest we move on, back to the brighter edge of the park, where we can see the tower blocks, turning our exit from the canopy into a chasing game in order to move things along.

As I duck my way out beneath one of the young oaks I am struck by the strangeness of its acorns, which don't look like acorns at all but, rather, as if a molten acorn had been frozen in mid-explosion. Later I google something along the lines of *weird acorns* and find immediately an answer to these tiny explosions decorating the branches of this small oak. They are called knopper galls and are the result of a certain gall wasp laying its eggs in developing acorns, to which the tree responds with these wild, bright green growths which house the larvae where each acorn might have been. They are apparently harmless.

As we leave along the edge path of the cemetery park, shadowed by flats on one side, I watch the bright black of bees and try to quell my profound unease at the strangeness of each improbable knopper gall and the dead, some centuries buried, still signalling their presence.

And it still happens, all the time—my hands are not my own as I watch them touch him. That quiet catastrophe and its shortened breath, its slowing of time, the sense of falling and panic and horror, the fizz of fear just beneath my scalp. And then the going on, but with the loss reinforced each time, I think.

Eventually we arrive at the sea, or rather at the slope of a seaside town. Amara left and came back, well back to the county, a long way really from where we grew up, but still. Now she's a *DFL* (Down From London). We were at school together and now, as I reach her new home, two minutes from the small station, our young sons play a greeting game of hide and seek that performs their excitement and nervousness at seeing each other again after a few months. I am overjoyed to see her.

At the slow pace of transitioning from one place to another with small children, we make our way for fish and chips, and then my son has stripped to his pants and is running into the low, foamed waves as I wade beside him, my trousers rolled up to my knees but soaked still, making sure he isn't swept away.

His is a total abandon, even in the face of a force so tremendous as the sea, and he looks smaller than ever as waves break right up to his shoulders and he must be tasting salt. The beach is busy but once our feet are in the water, feeling its surge and pull, this doesn't matter.

I step off the train and think *I want to close the rawness of my heart.*
But I need to say more or you won't understand.

My movements are taut and clumsy, missing their mark, my hands a little numb. I wonder if I really explained this at the start. Because now all I can think about is how this is what it was like, some of the time, when he was a baby.

Now it is because we are weeks into the summer holidays and I have so little respite from the labour of care. We have mostly wonderful days, outside, exploring, but I have only time for sleep, no rest, and my body is rebelling against this outrage.

I keep remembering your eyes, because I can't remember your actual words. You were telling me how hard it had been, what a dark time, raising your daughter on your own, yourself just 18, in the small Scottish town where you had grown up. Some small chunk of that darkness passed into me as you tried to make me understand what I could not possibly comprehend, standing awkwardly in a London pub amid a crowd of your friends, celebrating an exhibition of your sculpture at a gallery around the corner, years before I would have a child myself.

But I knew there was something important there, in your eyes. Not a warning exactly, just a significance that needed to be shared, even with an almost-stranger as I was. Your daughter was grown now, at university, but still, even on this night, the pain of those early years, alone, was something you chose to talk about.

That small piece of darkness that you passed to me stayed with me, waiting, until now, when I have the experience to understand it, partially of course, as all things are understood. I turn it in the light now and I think of it as having the dark translucence of flint.

I wish you were telling me now so, in return for the small piece of dark flint, I could show you that I understand, more at least than I did then, young, awkward, awed and drawn to you, so that of course you seemed impossible, unreal, even in your frankness.

He steals red apples from the crates beneath the fruit and veg stall. Gleeful and overexcited as I hand him a coin which he offers to the farmer, in exchange for the already part-eaten fruit. Always apples, and *red* he insists. As if he knows his apple scrumping ancestry, his great and great great grandparents' poaching of fallen fruit, not just in childhood but all their lives, long after they could afford to buy them, in Kentish orchards, a-buzz with drunken wasps, perhaps.

We take his apple past the other stalls of the small market, through the city farm's courtyard, and into the *forest garden*, a few square feet of bucolic dell. We sit beneath a tree's hanging branches and I cannot stop smiling at this small wonder of green.

We used to be able to walk through the allotments too and wonder at the beds, like rows of moored fishing boats with various constructions of wood and net atop each raised bed, but the gate is chained these days.

But the city farm is a generous place and one of the volunteers offers him a go watering the plants with the hose, which he takes without knowledge that such generosity is not commonplace.

The sound of the bedroom door against the doorstop, like a deep crunching of ice. He only hears this sound in his sleep, and I wonder if, one day, when he is an adult, he will hear the same noise and wonder why it resonates in his bones with something like a memory—of falling and containment, of the warm skin smell of sheets and the weight of his hot legs and motionless arms.

ACKNOWLEDGEMENTS

For C, for making me a writer, a mother and so much more.

For J and R, for their love and support, and for being the family I choose.

For my beautiful friends.

With heartfelt thanks to Meg Jensen and Sara Upstone at Kingston University, for their invaluable input on earlier versions of this text.

Thank you to each of the editors, conference and exhibition organisers who have given me the chance to put my words out into the world, and to each of the readers/listeners who have shown me why this is worthwhile.

Thank you to my Kingston PhD and teaching colleagues, particularly in the Race/Gender Matters research group, for reading and responding to work in progress.

With endless gratitude to Aaron Kent for choosing to publish this work, and for all the amazing books that Broken Sleep sets out into the world.

For all those trying to mother 'otherwise'.

LAY OUT YOUR UNREST